# ESCORT CARRI

## in action

By Al Adcock
Color by Don Greer
Illustrated by Joe Sewell

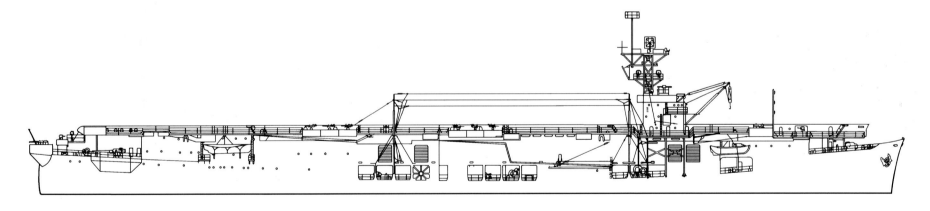

**Warships Number 9**

**squadron/signal publications**

The USS GUADALCANAL (CVE-60) and the ships and aircraft of her Task Group captured the German U-boat U-505, the only submarine captured by a carrier during the entire war. The GUADALCANAL earned a Presidential Unit Citation for this action. The U-505 is currently on display at the Museum of Science and Industry in Chicago.

# Camouflage

Escort carriers were camouflaged in various paint schemes known as Measures. The Measure schemes were designed to provide the maximum amount of concealment under the types of conditions that the ships were to operate under. Ships of the U.S. Navy have been painted in many schemes from the Great White Fleet to the Black & White Dazzle schemes designed to confuse the observer.

During the Second World War, the U.S. Fleet operated mainly in the Atlantic and Pacific and these areas required different camouflage schemes. Due to light conditions another scheme was required for the North Atlantic area. The Navy took a page from the British and used paint schemes developed during the First World War by the Admiralty for use in convoy duties in that area. During 1943-44, U.S. schemes for the North Atlantic were either Measure 17, 32, or 33 and various sub-systems of the Measure 32/33 camouflage system, some of which were specifically tailored for individual ships, like Measure 32/15a designed for the USS MARCUS ISLAND (CVE-77). Measure 21 was also used in the Atlantic beginning in 1943 through 1945.

In the Pacific, Measure 14 and 22 as well as Measure 32 and 33, were employed. Dazzle schemes used multiple colors in Blues, Grays and Purples. Measure 14 and 22 were solid colors of Gray or Blue.

For every rule there are exceptions, such as ships painted for the Atlantic serving in the Pacific and Pacific ships serving in the Atlantic.

ISBN 0-89747-356-6

If you have any photographs of aircraft, armor, soldiers or ships of any nation, particularly wartime snapshots, why not share them with us and help make Squadron/Signal's books all the more interesting and complete in the future. Any photograph sent to us will be copied and the original returned. The donor will be fully credited for any photos used. Please send them to:

Squadron/Signal Publications, Inc.
1115 Crowley Drive
Carrollton, TX 75011-5010

Если у вас есть фотографии самолётов, вооружения, солдат или кораблей любой страны, особенно, снимки времён войны, поделитесь с нами и помогите сделать новые книги издательства Эскадрон/Сигнал ещё интереснее. Мы переснимем ваши фотографии и вернём оригиналы. Имена приславших снимки будут сопровождать все опубликованные фотографии. Пожалуйста, присылайте фотографии по адресу:

Squadron/Signal Publications, Inc.
1115 Crowley Drive
Carrollton, TX 75011-5010

軍用機、装甲車両、兵士、軍艦などの写真を所持しておられる方はいらっしゃいませんか？どの国のものでも結構です。作戦中に撮影されたものが特に良いのです。Squadron/Signal社の出版する刊行物において、このような写真は内容を一層充実し、興味深くすることができます。当方にお送り頂いた写真は、複写の後お返しいたします。出版物中に写真を使用した場合は、必ず提供者のお名前を明記させて頂きます。お写真は下記にご送付ください。

Squadron/Signal Publications, Inc.
1115 Crowley Drive
Carrollton, TX 75011-5010

# Acknowledgements

U.S. Navy    Elsilrac Enterprises    National Museum of Naval Aviation
NASA    Todd Shipyards    Maja D. Larson
National Archives

A U.S. Navy K-ship overflies the USS BOUGE (CVE-9) in the Atlantic as the ship's TBM Avengers prepare for flight operations. The U.S. Navy used the escort carriers and blimps to hunt German submarines. The USS BOUGE was finished in Measure 22 camouflage. (Navy)

3

# Introduction

They were called Jeep Carriers, Woolworth Carriers, Kaisers Coffins, and many other names, some unprintable. But no matter what they were called, when they were called for duty, they performed tasks that enabled them and the larger American and British fleet aircraft carriers to take the fight to the enemy.

America's first experience with flying off of a ship occurred on 11 November 1910, when stunt pilot Eugene Ely, flying a Curtiss biplane, took off from the U.S. Navy scout cruiser USS BIRMINGHAM. Ely took off from USS BIRMINGHAM, anchored in Chesapeake Bay and flew to a airfield near the Norfolk Naval Base, Virginia. The Navy was not impressed, they called it merely a stunt. Ely didn't give up and two months later, after moving to the west coast, he convinced the Navy to loan him the cruiser USS PENNSYLVANIA. The Navy constructed a wooden deck on the stern and devised an arresting gear from rope and sandbags. Ely swooped in low over San Francisco Bay and landed on the PENNSYLVANIA, marking the first time than an aircraft had landed on a ship. Following lunch with the captain, Ely then turned the Curtiss around and took off. Again, the Navy was not impressed, they called it "a visit."

The event did not go unnoticed in England and Japan. The Royal Navy saw some promise in the design and began experiments along the lines of Ely's modified cruiser design during the First World War. In 1919, Japan began the construction of the small carrier HONSHO and the fledgling naval air arm of Japan began to grow. Due to international pressure to halt the arms race in ship construction, a conference was called in Washington D.C. during 1921, with the sole purpose of limiting capital ship and carrier tonnage. The actual reason for the Washington Conference was to limit the number of ships that Japan was building, which the western powers thought would put them at an unfair advantage in the event of a global war. Japan continued to build ships, but it would be another twenty years before Japan was strong enough to attack the American naval installation at Pearl Harbor, Hawaii.

America wouldn't build its first aircraft carrier until 1922, and then it was a converted collier, the 11,500 ton USS JUPITER. She had been commissioned during 1913, and was the Navy's first large turbo-electric driven ship. She was converted to the aircraft carrier role by placing a wooden flight deck over the hull. Once completed, she was re-commissioned as USS LANGLEY (CV-1). Vought VE-7SF aircraft were brought aboard and flight operations were soon under way. The VE-7SF was a modified gun-armed trainer that had a slow landing speed, just right for the burgeoning U.S. Naval Aviation Arm to train on. After a two year shake down, the LANGLEY was ready for action. Before the Second World War, LANGLEY was converted to a seaplane tender, with her flight deck shortened and reclassified as AV-3. During the Battle of the Java Sea in February of 1942, she was sunk by Japanese naval aviation forces while trying to bring much needed P-40 fighters to Java.

In late 1920, the keel was laid for the battle cruiser USS SARATOGA and during early 1922, the another battle cruiser, the USS LEXINGTON was laid down. Following the Washington Naval Conference, both were reordered as aircraft carriers and commissioned during late 1927, beginning the buildup of the carrier fleet for the U.S. Navy. But the buildup came at a very high price. The LEXINGTON cost over $44 million dollars, quite a bit for the time period. Due to the high cost of aircraft carriers, the Navy began searching for a smaller, more economical way to carry aircraft, both to protect the fleet and take the fight to the enemy, thus began the "flying deck cruiser" concept.

Eugene Ely became the first person to fly an aircraft off the deck of a ship. On 11 November 1910, Ely, flying a Curtiss biplane, took off from the make-shift flight deck that had been constructed on the bow of the cruiser USS BIRMINGHAM. (Elsilrac)

Following his successful take-off from the USS BIRMINGHAM, Ely convinced the Navy to construct a landing deck on the cruiser USS PENNSYLVANIA (CA-4). When the deck was completed Ely landed, becoming the first man to land an aircraft on a ship. (National Archives)

Ely takes off from the USS PENNSYLVANIA, anchored in San Francisco Bay, following what the Navy called a "visit on board." It would be over ten years before the Navy decided to construct a real aircraft carrier. Ely did, however, prove the feasibility of aircraft operating from ships at sea. (Elsilrac)

The idea was to build a ship 650 feet long, with the forward section for three triple mounted 6 inch guns and the after section for an angled 350 foot long flight deck and hanger area. The

The Russian KIEV Class was designed along the lines of the Flying Deck Cruiser, a design that combined the fighting capabilities of a cruiser and a flight deck for aircraft operations. The KIEV Class operates helicopters and vertical takeoff aircraft in the anti-submarine role. (Navy)

angled flight deck was a novel idea that didn't catch on in the U.S. Navy until 1952, when the USS ANTIETAM (CV-36) was fitted with an angle deck. The British were the first to adopt the angle deck for their fleet carriers. The "flying deck cruiser" was to carry twenty-four scout and fighter aircraft, but it was just an idea and no funding was forthcoming. By 1940 the project was dropped, with the option to look at the project in the future. The Germans and Japanese ended forever the concept with the start of the Second World War. The Soviet Union, during the 1960s, adopted a design that closely resembled the "flying deck cruiser" concept. The four ship KIEV class was designed for anti-submarine duties with helicopter and Yak 38 VTOL (vertical takeoff or landing).

On 1 September 1939, the German army attacked their neighbor, Poland, dragging, by

## Flying Deck Cruiser Concept

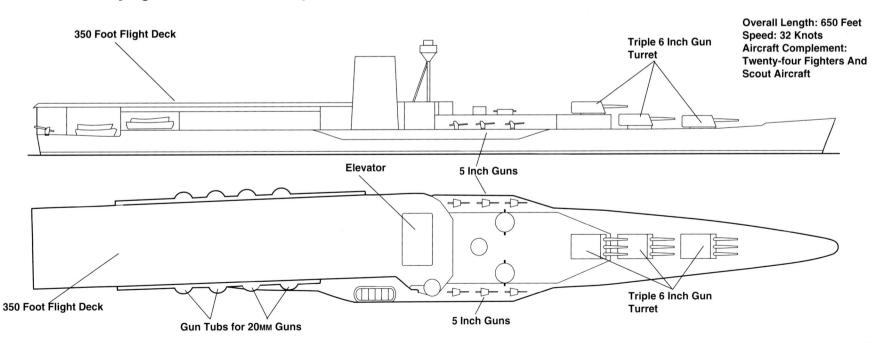

350 Foot Flight Deck

Triple 6 Inch Gun Turret

Overall Length: 650 Feet
Speed: 32 Knots
Aircraft Complement: Twenty-four Fighters And Scout Aircraft

Elevator

5 Inch Guns

350 Foot Flight Deck

Gun Tubs for 20MM Guns

5 Inch Guns

Triple 6 Inch Gun Turret

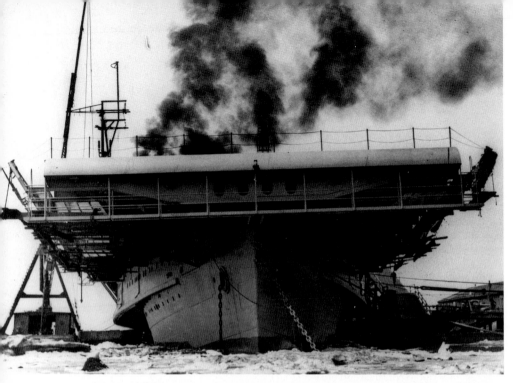

**The USS WOLVERINE (IX-64) and USS SABLE (IX-81) were both paddle wheel steamers converted to training carriers, proving that just about anything could be used for an aircraft carrier. Both served in Lake Michigan training Naval aviators. (Floating Drydock)**

treaty, the French and British into the war. As the war escalated, the British, now fighting alone after the fall of France, needed war material to protect their home island. This resulted in the Lend-lease Agreement, where U.S. goods were exchanged for base rights for U.S. forces on British soil. Britain needed all types of items to fight the Germans, from airplanes, oil, guns, and ammunition to clothing, food and most of all a way to transport it from America to England. Atlantic convoys were set up and war material began to flow from U.S. ports to Britain. To stem the tide of these war goods, the Germans employed their U-boats, hundreds of them in Wolf Packs. So effective were the U-boats that some thought was given to abandoning the convoy system and flying all material to England. That thought proved impractical and other methods were tried. Air cover for the convoys proved very effective, but the limited range of patrol aircraft left the convoys unprotected in the middle of the Atlantic. Plus, the Germans began employing long range Focke Wulf FW-200 Condors, against the Atlantic convoys. The only solution to this dilemma was to provide constant and continuous air cover over the complete convoy route. That meant that fighter and scout aircraft and a way to transport them. There weren't enough aircraft carriers available, so some solution was needed. Thus was born the idea of a escort carrier, a class of ship that could be constructed in a short period of time.

The first escort carrier to be constructed was built by the British and launched on 22 January 1941. Taking a page from the Americans with their LANGLEY design, they used the captured German passenger/cargo ship, HANNOVER as the basis for the escort carrier. With the addition of a flight deck and armament, the HMS AUDACITY was born. The life span of HMS AUDACITY, was very short. She was sunk by a German torpedo in December of 1941, after having served for only four months. the U.S. Navy was not far behind, the motorships MS MORMACMAIL and RIO DE LA PLATA were taken over by the Navy for conversion to escort carriers. The first, USS LONG ISLAND (AVG-1), was actually commissioned two weeks before HMS AUDACITY.

Escort carriers carried many designators during the war years. As originally acquired, on 6 March 1941, USS LONG ISLAND, the Navy's first escort carrier, was designated as an auxiliary ship and classified as AVG-1, for Aircraft Escort Vessel Auxiliary. On 20 August 1942, the classification was changed to ACV for Auxiliary Aircraft Carrier. Finally, on 15 July 1943, the classification CVE was bestowed on the escort carriers to recognize their status as true warships. The designator, CVE, stood for Escort Carrier Aircraft, but to those that served on them, they were C-combustible, V-vulnerable, E-expendable. All U.S. escort carriers carried the CVE classification throughout the balance of the war. Following the Korean War, the CVE's were again reclassified as CVUs or Utility Aircraft Carrier and those so modified to handle helicopters as CVHE, the H standing for Helicopter. When the USS THETIS BAY was extensively modified, she was classified as the first CVHA for Assault Helicopter Aircraft Carrier. THETIS BAY was further reclassified as an Amphibious Assault Ship, LHA, on 27 October 1955. The final reclassification of the remaining escort carriers saw their designators changed to AKV for Cargo Ship, Aircraft, their designations having come full circle.

American escort carriers were named for rivers, bays and famous battles in the Atlantic and Pacific, plus to honor the name of escort carriers lost in battle. A confusing array of names adorned the escort carriers. The lead ship in the CASABLANCA class was laid down as the British HMS AMEER, but since it was not delivered to Britain, she was renamed on 23 January 1943 to commemorate the Battle of the Coral Sea which took place during 1942. The name CORAL SEA was given to a new fleet carrier USS CORAL SEA (CVB-9) so the escort carrier was once again renamed, this time to USS CASABLANCA on 3 April 1945.

In 1942, with most of the allied escort carriers tied up with war duties, a need was realized for small aircraft carriers to train naval aviators. All large ships capable of being modified were in the works or on the building ways, too far along for practical conversion. The only large ships available were two side paddle wheel steamers, the GREATER BUFFALO and the SEA AND BEE. Conversion to the training carrier role involved the removal of the upper decks and the addition of a flight deck over the hull.

The flight decks were over 500 feet in length and only twenty-five feet above the water. A bridge was constructed on the starboard paddle wheel cover, mainly for realism. Once the conversion process was completed, the SEA AND BEE was commissioned as the USS WOLVERINE (1X-64) and the GREATER BUFFALO was commissioned as the USS SABLE (1X-81). Both ships operated in Lake Michigan, training pilots mainly from Naval Air Station Glenview, Illinois.

American escort carriers participated in every major naval campaign from Operation TORCH in November of 1942 to the fall of Japan in September of 1945. They hunted subs in the Atlantic and Pacific. They transported aircraft, aircraft parts, troops, and brought back the sick and wounded following hostilities. No job was to big or to small for the escort carriers, they handled them all. There were four Presidential Unit Citations awarded to U.S. aircraft carriers during the Second World War, three of them went to escort carriers.

# LONG ISLAND

The USS LONG ISLAND was originally laid down at the Sun Shipbuilding Company, Chester, Pennsylvania as the MS MORMACMAIL during 1940. On 6 March 1941 the U. S. Navy acquired the motor ship and sent her to Newport News Shipbuilding and Dry Dock, in Virginia for conversion to the first auxiliary heavier than air aircraft carrier (AVG) for the U. S. Navy. The conversion from motor ship to aircraft carrier took three months to complete and, upon completion, the MORMACMAIL was commissioned as the USS LONG ISLAND (AVG-1).

The LONG ISLAND, being a converted C3 cargo (m) freighter, was 492 feet in length and had a beam of 69.6 feet with a draught of 28.5 feet. She had a standard displacement of 7,886 tons and fully loaded displaced 13,500 tons. The power plant was a Sun-Doxford diesel that produced 8,500 hp and drove a single screw, which gave the USS LONG ISLAND a maximum rated speed of 16 knots.

As originally converted, the LONG ISLAND had a flight deck that did not extend over the bow boat deck. This short deck precluded the LONG ISLAND from operating any large aircraft from her deck. During the Fall of 1942, the flight deck was extended out over the boat deck, increasing the length by forty feet, bringing the overall length to 450 feet. With the extension of the flight deck, a catapult was added. A derrick was fitted to the port side flight deck to bring seaplanes aboard for servicing. One elevator was placed in the after flight deck area, about two-thirds down the deck

The USS LONG ISLAND was armed with one 5 inch 51 caliber deck gun (of the same type that had been carried by older U. S. battleships) mounted on the fantail. Two 3 inch 50 caliber weapons were placed on the bow and twenty 20MM anti-aircraft guns were placed along side the flight deck for close in protection.

In December of 1942, SC surface search radar was fitted to the newly installed mast on the starboard forward side of the flight deck. The square shaped antenna was replaced during 1944 by the upgraded rectangular SC-2 antenna, a YE aircraft homing antenna shared the mast.

Soon after commissioning, the LONG ISLAND was used to test the feasibility of operating aircraft from the decks of converted freighters. The Douglas SBD Dauntless was initially evaluated, but due to its size was never carried operationally. Following the evaluation, Scouting 201 (VS-201) was assigned in December of 1941. The squadron consisted of seventeen Curtiss SOC-3 Seagull biplane scouting aircraft that were fitted with fixed landing gear for carrier operations and seven Brewster F2A-3 Buffalo fighters. During the Summer of 1942, VGS-1, also equipped with F2As and SOCs, was assigned to the LONG ISLAND, but following that deployment, the LONG ISLAND was assigned the training role, qualifying naval aviators in carrier operations off the coast of California, or for transporting aircraft to forward bases in the Pacific.

During its career the, USS LONG ISLAND wore various camouflage paint schemes. During 1942 she carried Measure 12, a graded system that employed Sea Blue and Haze Gray with the deck being painted Deck Blue. Instead of the ship's number being painted on the deck, the initials LI were painted on the deck near the bow and stern. In late 1942, she was repainted in Measure 14, overall Ocean Gray. By 1944, the LONG ISLAND was finished in the Measure 32/9a scheme that was designed to confuse enemy observers. The 32/9a scheme used three colors of Gray.

The USS LONG ISLAND (CVE-1) was the former diesel powered motorship MORMAC-MAIL that was converted to become the first escort aircraft carrier for the U.S. Navy. The conversion to escort carrier took place at the Norfolk Naval Shipyard during 1941. As originally converted, the LONG ISLAND was fitted with a flight deck that did not extend over the forward boat deck. The White LI on the fore and after flight deck was the designator for the LONG ISLAND. Two Brewster F2A Buffalo fighters are spotted on the forward flight deck. (Elsilrac)

The LONG ISLAND's last service to the U. S. Navy was her participation in Operation MAGIC CARPET, bringing the troops home following the victory over Japan. The LONG ISLAND was then stricken from the U. S. Navy list on 26 March 1946. In 1949 she was converted, with the removal of her flight deck, to the motorship NEELY. In 1953, upon a change of ownership, she was renamed the SEVEN SEAS.

The USS LONG ISLAND at anchor with SOC-3 aircraft from VGS-1, her assigned squadron, on the flight deck. The LONG ISLAND was camouflaged in Measure 12, with splotches. The paint scheme was incomplete, with the after section of the hanger deck unfinished. Measure 12, as modified, was also employed by the USS WASP (CV-7) and USS HORNET (CV-8) during the early to mid-1942 time frame. The LONG ISLAND was the only U.S. escort carrier without a starboard island, the bridge was split into tubs on either side of the flight deck. (National Archives)

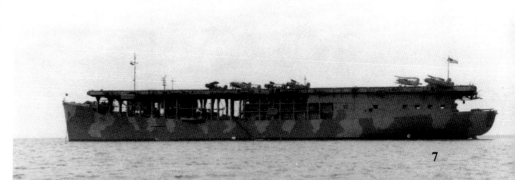

# USS LONG ISLAND

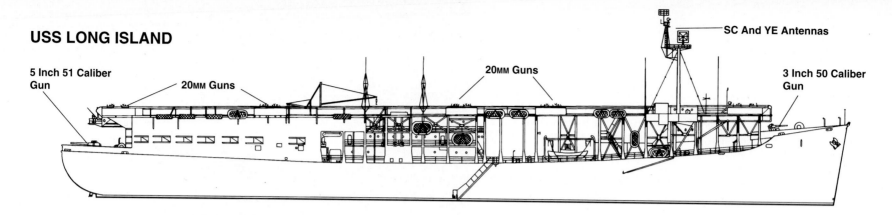

SC And YE Antennas

5 Inch 51 Caliber Gun

20MM Guns

20MM Guns

3 Inch 50 Caliber Gun

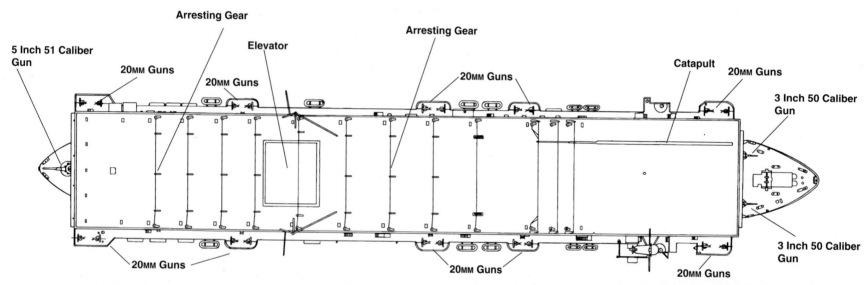

Arresting Gear

Elevator

Arresting Gear

Catapult

5 Inch 51 Caliber Gun

20MM Guns

20MM Guns

20MM Guns

20MM Guns

3 Inch 50 Caliber Gun

20MM Guns

20MM Guns

20MM Guns

3 Inch 50 Caliber Gun

The USS LONG ISLAND underwent a further conversion near the end of 1941 at Norfolk Navy Yard, adding a forty foot extension to the flight deck; which now went out over the forward boat deck. The LONG ISLAND sailed to the Pacific in mid-1942 for operations off the Gilbert Islands transporting Marine Corps SBD and TBF aircraft. (Navy)

The LONG ISLAND in Puget Sound during February of 1944. The USS LONG ISLAND served solely in the Pacific during the Second World War transporting aircraft, spares and personnel from the West Coast to the Pacific area. At the end of hostilities the LONG ISLAND participated in Operation MAGIC CARPET, bringing back American troops from the Pacific war zone, camouflaged in Measure 32/9a. (Navy)

8

# BOUGE Class

The BOUGE Class represented the first major build of escort carriers for the U. S. Navy and Great Britain. As in the LONG ISLAND, the BOUGE Class utilized the C-3 type cargo hull as the basis for the carriers. The BOUGE class was represented by twenty ships, ten for the U. S. Navy and ten for the Royal Navy. All U. S. Navy carriers were constructed by Todd Shipbuilding, Tacoma, Washington.

The first of the class, USS BOUGE was laid down as the STEEL ADVOCATE on 10 October 1941. She was taken over by the U. S. Navy a short time later and her conversion to escort carrier commenced. She was launched 15 January 1942 and commissioned as USS BOUGE (AVG-9) on 26 September 1942. The BOUGE class ships were essentially the same dimensions as her sister ships the USS LONG ISLAND and later USS CHARGER, with an overall length of 492 feet and a beam of 69.6 feet. The wood flight deck was 111.5 feet wide and was some fifty-four feet above the water. Her draught was 23.3 feet and displacement was rated at 7,800 standard tons and full load was 13,000 tons. The BOUGE Class differed from LONG ISLAND in that they were steam powered rather than diesel powered. The power plant used in the BOUGE Class was two Foster-Wheeler boilers, which fed two Westinghouse geared steam turbines driving a single screw. With 3,420 tons of bunker fuel, the BOUGE Class had a range of 8.000 miles when steaming at 15 knots.

Armament consisted of two new 5 inch 38 caliber guns mounted on sponsons on the aft

The USS BOUGE (CVE-9), sailing in the Atlantic during 1943, was camouflaged in Measure 22. The USS BOUGE was the first escort carrier used in the Atlantic in the hunter-killer role against German U-boats and her aircraft group sunk seven U-boats on their first cruise. The BOUGE was awarded a Presidential Unit Citation for her actions in the Atlantic. (Navy)

The BOUGE and PRINCE WILLIAM Class were constructed using C-3-S A1 cargo type hulls like the USS FREEMONT (APA-44). The 492 foot hulls were overlaid with a wooden flight deck and an island structure was placed on the starboard side of the deck for steering, navigational and flight operations needs. (Elsilrac)

By 1944, the USS BOUGE was camouflaged in Measure 32/4a. An Eastern Aircraft FM Wildcat had just landed on deck and was being directed forward. During 1944, the BOUGE was again participating in sub hunting in the Atlantic, along with a few other CVEs, as well as serving as a training platform for Navy air crews. (Navy)

lower hull, twenty twin 40MM Bofors anti-aircraft mounts and up to twenty-seven 20MM Oerlikon anti-aircraft guns fitted to various locations along the flight deck and island. One catapult was fitted to the port side flight deck adjacent to the forward aircraft elevator, with the exception of the USS BOUGE, USS CARD and USS CORE, which were fitted with two, one to port and one to starboard. The catapult equipment and machinery was housed in the number one cargo hold. Configured as an aircraft transport, the BOUGE Class could accommodate fifty aircraft on the flight deck and forty below on the hanger deck. For normal flight operations, up to twenty-four aircraft could be handled, normally split twelve F4F (FM) Wildcat fighters and twelve TBF (TBM) torpedo bombers in a composite squadron.

During the Second World War the BOUGE Class wore a variety of camouflage schemes depending on the year and area of operations. During 1942, the Ocean Gray system was applied to all ships in the class. During 1943, the USS BOUGE, CARD, CORE, BLOCK ISLAND, AND CROATAN were operating in the Atlantic and were painted in measure 22, the graded system. The USS COPAHEE, NASSAU, ALTAMAHA, and BRETON were operating in the Pacific and were finished in Measure 14 Ocean Gray system. Measure 32, pattern system, and Measure 33, Thayer system were used during 1944, and depending on which ocean they were sailing on, Measure 32/2a, 32/4a 32/12a or 33/2a was applied. 32/12a and 33/2a for the Pacific and 32/4a or for the Atlantic. By 1945, all were painted in Measure 21, the Navy Blue system.

The USS BOUGE, CARD, CORE, BLOCK ISLAND and CROATAN were all assigned to the Atlantic Fleet and used in the anti-submarine role from 1943 to 1945. During Atlantic operations, both USS BOUGE and USS CARD were awarded Presidential Unit Citations for actions against German U-boats. On her first Atlantic cruise, USS CARD's composite squadron VC-1 sank four U-boats. The USS BOUGE sank thirteen U-boats during her Atlantic operations. It was during one of the Atlantic sub hunting operations that the USS BLOCK ISLAND was torpedoed and sunk off the Canary Islands on 29 May 1944, by the German U-boat U-549. She was the only U. S. Navy escort carrier to be lost in the Atlantic campaign. The U-549 itself was sunk by the destroyer escort USS EUGENE E. ELMORE (DE-686) a few minutes after BLOCK ISLAND was hit.

The USS COPAHEE, NASSAU, ALTAMAHA, BARNES and BRETON were all assigned to the Pacific Fleet during the Second World War and used mainly for aircraft transport duties. Following the war, they were all called upon to transport U. S. servicemen back to the United States under Operation MAGIC CARPET.

One ship, USS BITER (BAVG-3), that had been loaned to Great Britain was returned to the U. S. Navy on 9 April 1945, and loaned to France on the same day. Named the DIXMUNDE, she was used by France as an aircraft transport, mainly to ferry aircraft to Indo-China. The DIXMUNDE was returned to the U. S. Navy and later destroyed during weapons tests during 1966.

The remaining ships of the BOUGE Class were put in the reserve fleet after the end of hostilities. In 1958, the USS CARD, CORE and BRETON were reactivated and classified as Aircraft Carrier Auxiliary (CVU) and used as aircraft and cargo transports. During 1959, they were again reclassified as Aircraft Transport (AKV), and at that time, the USS CROATAN joined them. They were put under the operational control of the Maritime Sea Transport Service (MSTS) and were operated by civilian crews. During the Vietnam War all four were used to transport aircraft and helicopters to South Vietnam. By 1972, all of the class had been withdrawn from service and broken up, four ships of the class having served for over thirty years.

**USS CARD (CVE-11) underway in the Atlantic with Grumman TBF torpedo bombers and F4F fighters of VC-1 on her flight deck, during early 1943. The CARD's aircraft sank eight U-boats during two Atlantic cruises. The CARD was camouflaged in Measure 22 during the 1942-1943 time frame. She would go on to serve with the Navy until 1970, transporting aircraft to Southeast Asia during the Vietnam war. The CARD was the first CVE to be awarded a Presidential Unit Citation. (Elsilrac)**

**The USS COPAHEE (CVE-12) in the Pacific during 1944. The COPAHEE served in the Pacific as an aircraft transport bringing fresh aircraft out to the larger carriers and land based combat units. The COPAHEE was camouflaged in Measure 32/12A, a paint scheme developed for the Pacific area of operations. (Elsilrac)**

USS COPAHEE tied up wharf side with a deck load of SBD Dauntless dive bombers bound for the Pacific war zone on 10 April 1944. The COPAHEE was laid down as the STEEL ARCHITECH, a C-3-S-A1 merchantman, but completed as a CVE. As an aircraft transport, the USS COPAHEE could accommodate fifty aircraft on deck and forty on the hanger deck. (National Archives)

The USS COPAHEE underway off Hunters Point, San Francisco, California during 1944. The camouflage was Measure 32/12a. The deck was covered with TBM Avengers, F4U Corsairs and at least one SB2C Helldiver bound for the Pacific. Measure 32/12a consisted of Dull Black, Ocean Gray and Light Gray. All of the BOUGE Class ships were 492 feet in length. (Navy)

## BOUGE Class, USS COPAHEE (CVE-12)

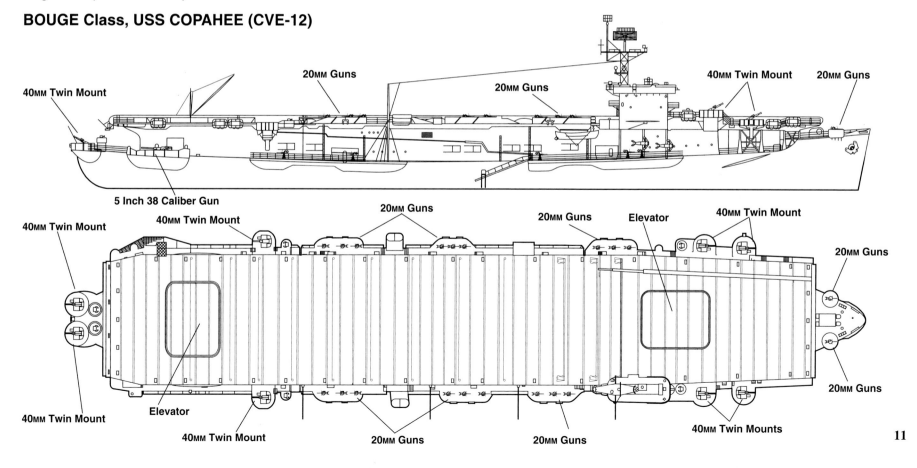

40MM Twin Mount

20MM Guns

20MM Guns

40MM Twin Mount

20MM Guns

5 Inch 38 Caliber Gun

40MM Twin Mount

40MM Twin Mount

20MM Guns

20MM Guns

Elevator

40MM Twin Mount

20MM Guns

Elevator

40MM Twin Mount

40MM Twin Mount

20MM Guns

20MM Guns

40MM Twin Mounts

Camouflage Measure 33/2a shows up well on the USS NASSAU (CVE-16). The NASSAU spent the Second World War in the Pacific transporting aircraft, providing a flight deck for pilot training and providing air cover for supply transports. (Elsilrac)

USS ALTAMAHA (CVE-18) underway in the Pacific during 1944. The deck was loaded with a cargo of North American P-51Bs and a solitary Naval Aircraft Factory SON-3 bound for the Pacific campaign. The ALTAMAHA served in the Pacific providing air cover, anti-submarine protection and aircraft transport. She was finished in camouflage Measure 14, a Dark Gray paint scheme. (Elsilrac)

The USS BLOCK ISLAND (CVE-21) underway in the Atlantic during 1943. The BLOCK ISLAND was finished in camouflage Measure 22. The BLOCK ISLAND sank two German U-boats during her 1943 cruise, but on 29 May 1944, she was sunk by a German U-boat off the coast of Africa. (Elsilrac)

USS BARNES (CVE-20) underway with a deck load of P-38 Lightnings and P-47 Thunderbolts bound for the Pacific area. The wings of the P-38s have been removed and stored on the hanger deck to conserve space and allow more aircraft to be carried. The BARNES served her entire career in the Pacific transporting aircraft and supplies to the Pacific area. (Elsilrac)

The USS BRETON (CVE-23) moored to the outfitting pier at the Seattle-Tacoma Shipyard, Tacoma, Washington on 1 February 1943. The USS BRETON served the entire war time period with Carrier Transport Squadron, Pacific. Following the Second World War the USS BRETON was put in the reserve fleet. In 1958, she was recalled and used in the Maritime Sea Transport Service (MSTS) transporting aircraft to Southeast Asia and Japan. (National Archives)

The USS BRETON (CVE-23) moving at speed in the Pacific during 1945, with the arresting gear undergoing maintenance by the deck crew. The BRETON was finished in camouflage Measure 21, the Navy Blue system. (Elsilrac)

A nearly complete USS BLOCK ISLAND (CVE-21) sits pier-side at the Seattle-Tacoma Shipyard during 1943. Measure 22 camouflage has been applied in preparation for duty in the Atlantic. Upon acceptance by the Navy, the BLOCK ISLAND was sailed though the Panama Canal to the Atlantic. (Navy)

The USS BRETON rides at anchor in San Francisco Bay on 10 May 1943. Her Measure 14 paint scheme shows the wear of at sea operations in the Pacific. SG, SC and YE radar antennas are fitted to the mast and a radar reflector flys at the halyard. (Navy)

The USS CORE (CVE-13) rides at anchor while fitting out at Seattle-Tacoma Shipyard, Washington on 24 January 1943. A Measure 22 camouflage paint scheme has been applied, even though the CORE would be used outside the combat zone for pilot qualifications. The CORE would later go on to serve in the Atlantic in the hunter/killer role. (Elsilrac)

USS CROATAN (CVE-25) at anchor during 1943, carries Measure 22 camouflage. The USS CROATAN along with her escorts sank two German U-boats during her 1944 Atlantic cruise. The USS CROATAN, like all her sisters, were constructed by Todd-Tacoma Shipyards, Washington. (Elsilrac)

The USS CROATAN (CVE-25) at sea in the Atlantic during 1943 with part of VC-19, her composite squadron of TBMs and FMs, on deck. The CROATAN would serve in the Atlantic for the balance of the Second World War. Following the war she was placed in reserve and during 1964 she was loaned to NASA for rocket experiments. Following that duty she was placed in service with MSTS as an aircraft ferry to Southeast Asia. (Elsilrac)

# SANGAMON Class

When adequate supplies of C-3 cargo ship hulls became unavailable, the U. S. Navy turned to tanker hulls to fulfill the need for additional escort carriers.

The first two, of four, SANGAMON Class escort carriers were laid down at the Federal-Kearny Shipyard as the ESSO TRENTON and MARKAY during 1939. The ESSO TRENTON and MARKAY were two of twelve national defense tankers ordered in 1939 and they all employed the TS-S2-A1 type oiler hulls. In 1940, all the oilers were taken over by the Navy and classified as fleet oilers in the CIMARRON Class. The second two in the class were built as the ESSO NEW ORLEANS AND SEAKAY at Sun Shipbuilding. As oilers they had a capacity of six million gallons of aviation gasoline.

During 1942, the USS SANGAMON (AO-28), CHENANGO (AO-31) and SUWANEE (AO-33) were all reclassified as AVGs upon commencement of their conversion to aircraft escort vessels. Newport News Shipbuilding and Drydock, Newport News, Virginia, converted the USS SANGAMON (AVG-26) and USS SUWANEE (AVG-27), while Bethlehem, Staten Island, New York, converted the USS CHENAGO (AVG-28) and the Norfolk Navy Yard, Norfolk, Virginia, converted the USS SANTEE (AVG-29).

SANGAMON Class ships were 553 feet long, with a beam of seventy-five feet and a draught of thirty feet six inches. The flight deck was 503 feet in length and eighty-one feet wide. It contained two elevators and one catapult. During refit in 1944, a second catapult was added to allow the ships to get more aircraft into the air quicker.

The class had a standard displacement of 12,000 tons, with 23,875 tons fully loaded. The power plant consisted of four boilers that supplied steam to geared turbines, producing 13,500 horse power, that drove twin screws, giving the ships a flank speed of 18 plus knots. The

**The USS SANGAMON (AO-28) was the former ESSO TRENTON that was taken over by the Navy before the Second World War. The USS SANGAMON and three of her sister CIMARRON class fleet oilers were converted to escort carriers in time to see action in Operation TORCH, the invasion of North Africa in November of 1942. (Floating Drydock)**

SANGAMON Class had a range of over 12,000 miles at 15 knots. Being former oilers, the machinery spaces were located aft, allowing for a larger below deck hanger space. The aviation fuel capacity was also greatly increased because of their oiler ancestry. A complement of 1,080 men were required to operate the ships of the SANGAMON Class.

The SANGAMON Class were fitted with three types of radar; surface search, air search and an aircraft homing beacon. During 1942, the SC type air search radar was installed and, by 1944, an improved SC-2 antenna was placed on the mast. For surface search, the SG antenna was utilized throughout the war. To a lost pilot, perhaps the most important radar antenna was the YE, aircraft homing beacon. The YE was, like the SG, used throughout the war.

Defensive armament originally consisted of three 5 inch 51 caliber mounts, two 1.1 inch anti-aircraft mounts, eight 40MM quad mounts, four 40MM twin mounts and twenty-one 20MM close in anti-aircraft weapons. The 5 inch 51 weapons were eventually replaced by the newer 5 inch 38 caliber Mark 21 Mod 0 guns. The 5 inch 51 weapons had been fitted to some of the older classes of battleships as secondary armament. All SANGAMON Class ships had their defensive armament increased to combat the Kamikaze attacks that began during 1944 in the Pacific, eventually reaching a total of twenty-eight 40MM anti-aircraft guns.

A total of thirty-five aircraft could be carried, but the usual complement was thirty. These ships normally operated Grumman F4F Wildcat and F6F Hellcat fighters along with TBF Avenger torpedo bombers. Eastern FM-2 Wildcats often replaced the F4Fs and occasionally they also carried SBD Dauntless dive bombers (the only class of escort carrier to operate SBDs). The aircraft were assigned to either air groups or squadrons depending on time period and tasks to be performed.

The usual aircraft complement was nine SBDs, twelve F6Fs, and nine TBF/TBMs. Alternate loads included eighteen F4Fs, nine SBDs and eight TBF/TBMs. During Operation TORCH, the invasion of North Africa in November of 1942, the flight deck and hanger deck of USS CHENANGO was covered with U. S. Army Air Corps Curtiss P-40 Warhawk land-based fighters. Using the catapult, the P-40s were launched and used as fighter cover for the invasion, before landing on captured airfields. The other SANGAMON Class ships operating in the task force carried their usual air complement of F4Fs, SBDs and TBFs.

Shortly after she was commissioned, USS SANGAMON (AVG-26) was used to conduct deck trials of the new Chance-Vought F4U Corsair. These tests were deemed unsuccessful, keeping the Corsair from flying off any U. S. Navy aircraft carrier until December of 1944. Although deck tests were on going by the Navy to correct the Corsairs deck handling problems in an attempt to qualify the F4U, the Royal Navy began carrier air operations with their Corsairs as early as 1943, including operations from their lend-lease CVEs.

During their operational careers the SANGAMON class were painted in various camouflage schemes. The colors ranged from the early Measure 14, known as the Ocean Gray system to the multi-colored 33/10a light pattern system. All of the paint systems were designed to confuse enemy aerial and naval observers under all lighting conditions. Of course it was a difficult task to hide a 500 foot long aircraft carrier in the middle of the ocean.

Operationally, the SAGAMONS first entered combat during late 1942. Their combat career lasted throughout the Second World War in both the Atlantic and Pacific theaters. Following the invasion of North Africa, the SANGAMON, SUWANEE and CHENAGO were transferred to the Pacific, where they usually operated as a team. The USS SANTEE stayed in the Atlantic, along with the USS CARD (CVE-11) AND USS CORE (CVE-13), hunting German submarines during 1943. Following her successful sub hunting career in the Atlantic SANTEE was sent to the Pacific in early 1944 to join her three sisters. The four SANGAMON

Class ships were used during the island hopping battles that took back the Pacific islands from Imperial Japanese forces.

All of the SANGAMON Class ships were damaged, either by operational accidents, as in the case of the USS CHENANGO, or by Kamikaze attack. The USS SANGAMON was damaged by just such an attack on 4 May 1945, while operating off Okinawa. The USS SUWANEE was damaged severely by Japanese dive bombers during the Battle of Samar, the Philippines in October of 1944. The damage was so severe that she had to return to the west coast for extensive repairs. The USS SANTEE was also damaged during this same battle by aerial and submarine launched torpedoes. She had her damage repaired at the Pearl Harbor Naval Base, Hawaii.

SANGAMON Class ships saw more action than any other class of escort carriers during the Second World War. The fact that they were larger, contained the deck space to handle more aircraft, carried more fuel and were much more seaworthy, all entered into the decision to utilize these ships to their fullest capability.

**The USS SANGAMON (CVE-26) was converted from the USS SANGAMON (AO-28), a tanker that had been taken over by the Navy during 1941. The conversion from tanker to escort carrier commenced on 14 April 1942, at Newport News Shipbuilding, Newport News, Virginia and she was recommissioned on 25 August 1942. The deck of USS SANGAMON was covered with F4Fs of VGF-26, plus TBFs and SBDs of VGS-26, destined for action in Operation TORCH, the invasion of North Africa. (Elsilrac)**

USS SUWANEE (CVE-27) at sea in October of 1943 off of Mare Island, California. The SUWANEE was finished in camouflage Measure 14, the Ocean Gray system. The lines of her fleet oiler ancestry are evident since she was the former tanker MARKAY converted to an escort carrier in early 1942, in time for the invasion of North Africa. (Navy)

The USS SUWANEE (CVE-27) at anchor in the Pacific off the Gilbert Islands during late 1943. Her air group consisted of VF-60 with F6Fs and VC-60 with SBDs and TBFs. The SUWANEE and her three sisters were participants in most of the major allied invasions during the Second World War. SG, SC and YE radar antennas are fitted to the mast. (Elsilrac)

## SANGAMON Class, USS SANGAMON (CVE-26)

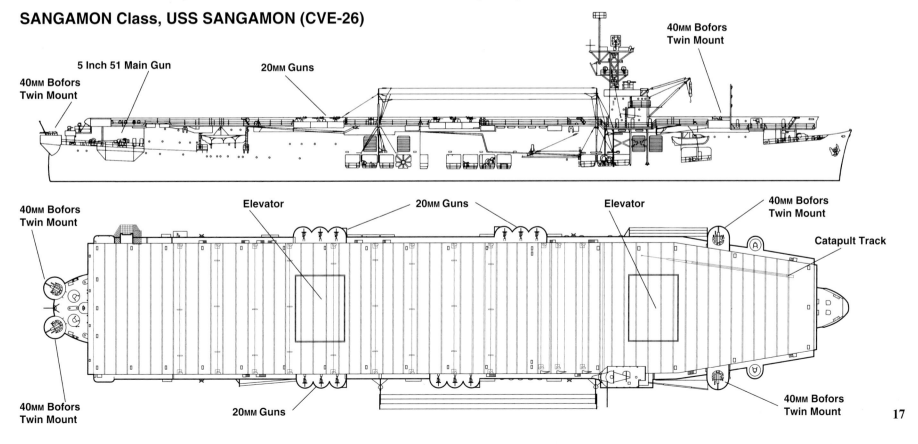

The USS SUWANEE underway at high speed in the Pacific in early 1943, soon after the invasion of North Africa. The 7 on the after flight deck was the designator for CVE-27. One could only wonder how many pilots from the USS WASP (CV-7) thought they were seeing a ghost, since the WASP had been sunk some four months earlier. (LCDR Charles Kerlee via National Archives)

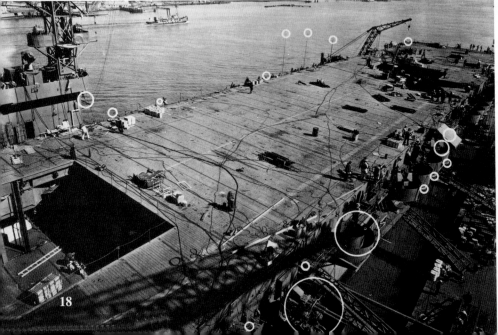

(Left) USS SUWANEE at Mare Island, California on 11 October 1943 during an overhaul period. The White circles indicate the many changes that were made to the flight deck and island area. Following the overhaul, USS SUWANEE participated in the invasions of the Gilbert Islands, Tarawa, and Makin Islands. The SANGAMON class CVEs could accommodate up to thirty-five aircraft when operating with a air group. (Navy)

USS CHENANGO (CVE-28) moves at slow speed before undergoing overhaul at Mare Island, California, during September of 1943. By October she was involved in the invasion of the Gilbert Islands. USS CHENANGO was the former tanker ESSO NEW ORLEANS converted by Bethlehem, Staten island, New York to an escort carrier. (Navy)

USS CHENANGO sailing out of Mare Island, California, on 22 September 1943. The CHENANGO and all her sisters had an advantage over the other converted escort carriers in that they had extra oil and gasoline tankage, being converted oilers. They operated as both carriers and tankers during the invasion of North Africa. (Navy)

The oiler ESSO NEW ORLEANS undergoes conversion to the escort carrier USS CHENANGO in September of 1942 at Bethlehem, Staten island, New York. The quad 1.1 inch gun mounts are visible on both sides of the flight deck. In the background is the builders ways of Bethlehem, Staten Island, New York. (Navy)

USS CHENANGO at anchor during early 1943, soon after being deployed to the Pacific for the invasion of the Gilbert Islands. The tanker conversions were more successful than the CVEs built from cargo hulls since they had more room available for hanger space amidships. All of the SANGAMON class were 553 feet in length and the flight deck was equipped with two aircraft elevators. (Elsilrac)

A F4F-4 named ROSENBLATT'S REPLY is readied for takeoff from the USS SUWANNEE (CVE-27) during late 1942. The aircraft still has traces of the Yellow national insignia surround. The size of the Grumman Wildcat made it perfect for operations from the smaller escort carrier flight deck. Wildcats would serve on the decks of all U.S. Navy escort carriers. (National Archives)

USS CHENANGO sailing out of Mare Island during late 1943. Once at sea, USS CHENANGO would begin receiving her aircraft for the invasion of the Gilbert Islands. The SANGAMON Class were the most heavily armed of the escort carriers. (Navy)

U.S. Army Air Corps Curtiss P-40F Warhawk fighters crowd the hangar deck of the USS CHENANGO. The Army fighters were being ferried to North Africa as part of the Operation TORCH invasion force. Once the invasion began the P-40s were brought on deck and catapulted off. They were flown to an airfield at Port Lyautey, Morocco. A total of seventy-eight P-40s had been carried to the war zone by USS CHENANGO. (Elsilrac)

## Aircraft Assigned To CVEs

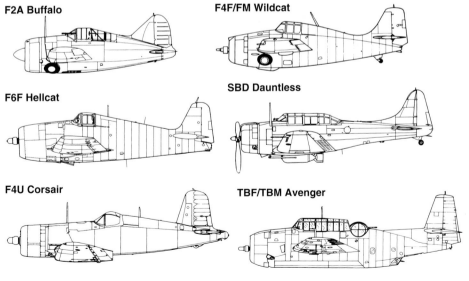

F2A Buffalo

F4F/FM Wildcat

F6F Hellcat

SBD Dauntless

F4U Corsair

TBF/TBM Avenger

21

The USS SANTEE (CVE-29) was the only escort carrier of the SANGAMON Class to use Measure 17 camouflage, a scheme that was the same on both port and starboard. The SANTEE saw action during the invasion of North Africa. She was the former tanker ESSO SEAKEY and had been converted to an escort carrier at the Norfolk Navy Yard, Norfolk, Virginia. (Navy)

The USS SANTEE in company with another SANGAMON Class CVE enroute to North Africa during late October 1942. The deck load consisted of fourteen F4Fs of VGF-29 and VGS-29, along with nine SBDs and eight TBFs for a total of thirty-one aircraft. (National Archives)

# CHARGER Class

By 1940, the war in Europe was raging and the British faced a pressing need for aircraft carriers and airmen to protect the home islands and the sea lines of communications. The Lend-lease treaty between England and the United States exchanged English land, needed for U.S. air bases, for U.S. ships and aircraft so desperately required for the British war effort.

The USS CHARGER, like her sister, the USS LONG ISLAND, was a former C-3 cargo ship, although the CHARGER was a C-3 passenger/cargo (diesel) type. CHARGER was converted from the former motor ship RIO DE LA PLATA that had been built by Sun Shipbuilding during 1940. In 1941, the U.S. Navy took over the ship and sent her to Newport News Shipbuilding for conversion to an Aircraft Carrier auxiliary. The conversion took seventy-seven days to complete and once completed the ship was taken over by the British and renamed HMS CHARGER (BAVG-4). The CHARGER did not remain in service with the Royal Navy for very long. On 4 October 1941, the CHARGER was returned to the U.S. to be used to train Royal Navy aviators. She retained her British name, but was reclassified as AVG-30 and recommissioned on 3 March 1942.

The USS CHARGER was 492 feet long, with a 450 foot flight deck. Her beam and draught were 69.6 and 25.2 feet respectively, while standard displacement was rated at 8,000 tons and fully loaded she displaced 15,126 tons. The CHARGER was powered by a 8,500 horse power Busch-Sulzer diesel that drove a single screw, giving the ship a rated speed of 16 knots and a range of 5,000 nautical miles. Armament consisted of one 5 inch 51 caliber gun mounted in a gun tub on the fantail, two 3 inch 50 caliber guns mounted in the bow area and twenty 20MM anti-aircraft guns placed along on either side of the flight deck. Not including the aircrews, the CHARGER had a ship's company of 856 men and officers.

The USS CHARGER differed from her sister, USS LONG ISLAND, in that she was fitted with an island structure on the starboard side. LONG ISLAND only had a navigational station on the forward edge of the flight deck. The CHARGER also had a longer flight deck, as originally built, a larger hanger area and aircraft repair shops that occupied the aft third of the ship. One aircraft catapult was provided abeam the island structure.

The USS CHARGER spent the entire war training British aviators in U.S. waters. The CHARGER operated in the Chesapeake Bay area with a few training cruises to Bermuda, Cuba and Florida. She could handle aircraft as large as the Douglas TBD Devastator and Grumman TBF Avenger on her deck to train the British airmen.

The CHARGER was camouflaged in Measure 22, the graded system, during most of her time in U.S. Navy service. Measure 22 was designed for use in areas where bright weather and fair to good visibility was usually present. The CHARGER was withdrawn from service following the Second World War and stricken on 15 March 1946.

Following the war, CHARGER was converted to the motorship FANSEA. The conversion included the removal of the flight deck and the addition of a cargo type superstructure.

**Shipyard workers prepare the USS CHARGER for service at the Norfolk Navy Shipyard, Portsmouth, Virginia during 1942. The CHARGER had just been returned to the U.S. Navy after a tour of service with the British Royal Navy. The SC radar antenna was the only antenna carried on the mast at this time. (Navy)**

**The USS CHARGER (CVE-30) gets underway with the aid of a tug during trials in the Atlantic, on 15 April 1942 off Norfolk, Virginia. The USS CHARGER was the former RIO DE LA PLATA converted to an escort carrier by the addition of a flight deck and associated flight deck gear. The CHARGER was transferred to the Royal Navy as the HMS CHARGER (BAVG-4) in 1941, but was returned later in the year to the U.S. Navy. (Navy)**

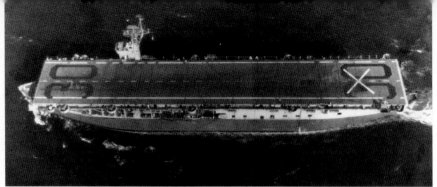

USS CHARGER being maneuvered in Chesapeake Bay in preparation for docking in Norfolk, Virginia. The USS CHARGER was used in the Atlantic to train British air and deck crews. The catapult track is the dark line on the forward port flight deck. The British, like the Americans used North American SNJ trainers for carrier qualifications. (National Archives)

The X superimposed on the flight deck numbers on the stern of USS CHARGER indicates that the flight deck is not usable for landings. The CHARGER was camouflaged in Measure 22, the graded system, that was used in the Atlantic during the 1942-43 time frame. The CHARGER was capable of handling twenty-one aircraft for training. (National Archives)

## CHARGER Class, USS CHARGER (CVE-30)

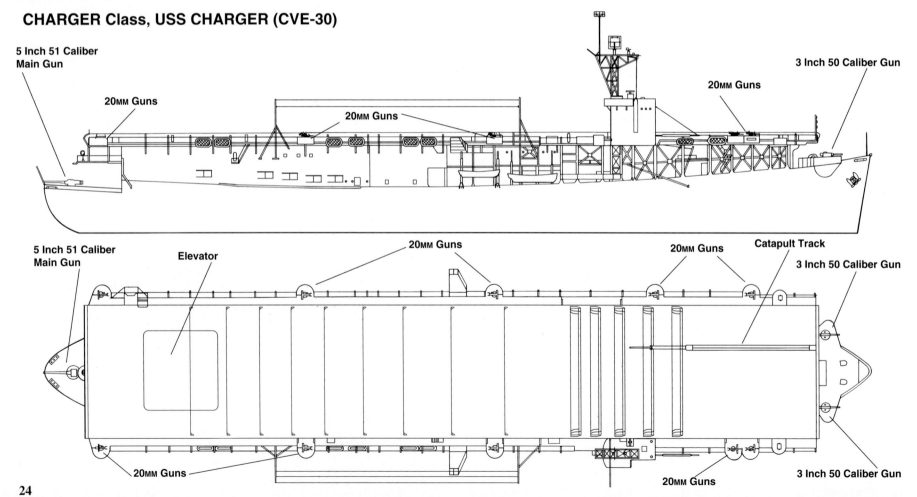

5 Inch 51 Caliber Main Gun

20mm Guns

20mm Guns

20mm Guns

3 Inch 50 Caliber Gun

5 Inch 51 Caliber Main Gun

Elevator

20mm Guns

20mm Guns

Catapult Track

3 Inch 50 Caliber Gun

20mm Guns

20mm Guns

3 Inch 50 Caliber Gun

The USS LONG ISLAND (AVG-1) was the former motorship MORMACMAIL converted to a carrier by the addition of a flight deck. She was camou-flaged in modified Measure 12.

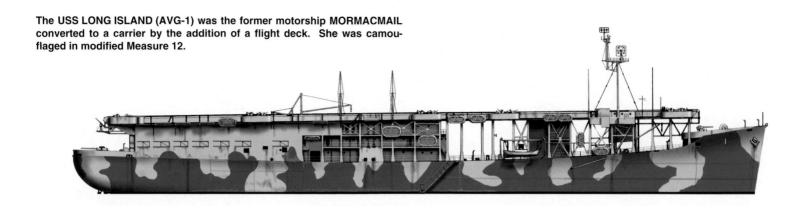

USS BLOCK ISLAND (CVE-21) was sunk during 1944 by a German U-boat while operating in the Atlantic. She was finished in Measure 22, a two tone Gray graded camouflage in use during 1943.

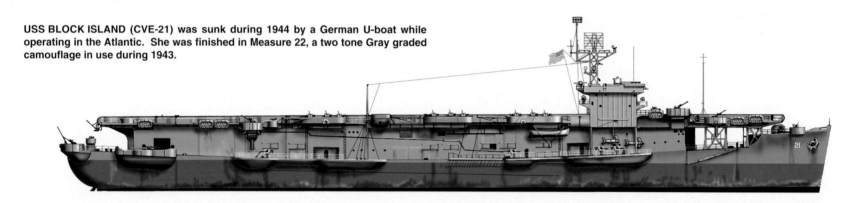

USS SANTEE (CVE-29) was finished in Measure 17 camouflage during September of 1942. This scheme was the same on either side.

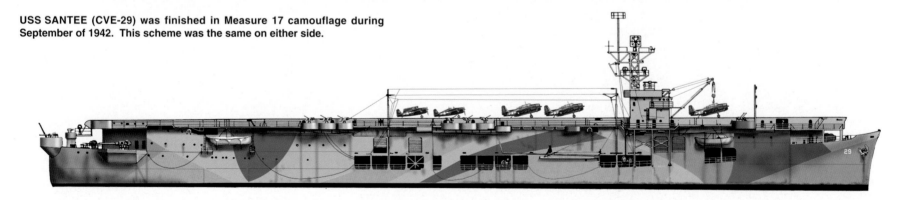

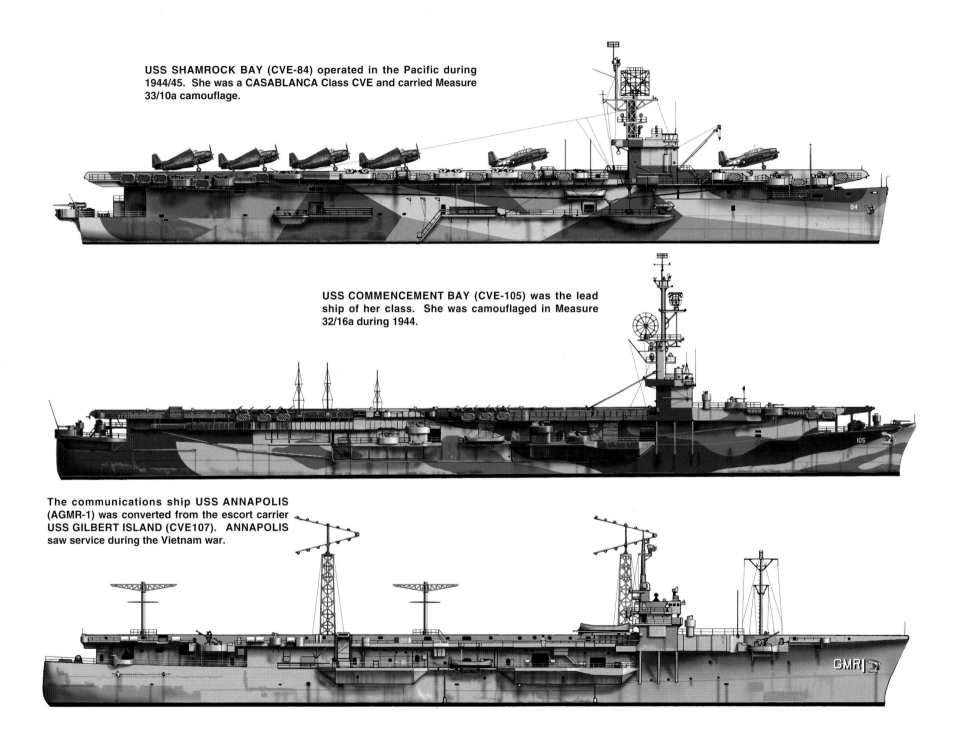

USS SHAMROCK BAY (CVE-84) operated in the Pacific during 1944/45. She was a CASABLANCA Class CVE and carried Measure 33/10a camouflage.

USS COMMENCEMENT BAY (CVE-105) was the lead ship of her class. She was camouflaged in Measure 32/16a during 1944.

The communications ship USS ANNAPOLIS (AGMR-1) was converted from the escort carrier USS GILBERT ISLAND (CVE107). ANNAPOLIS saw service during the Vietnam war.

# PRINCE WILLIAM Class

The PRINCE WILLIAM Class of escort carriers was a second batch of BOUGE Class ships and there were twenty-four ships in the class. One went to the U.S. Navy, one to the Royal Canadian Navy and twenty-two to the Royal Navy. The one Canadian ship was the HMCS NABOB (CVE-41). The NABOB remained under the control of the Royal Navy, but was classified as a U.S. naval vessel. Once in British service, the ships were known as the RULER Class. The lead ship, HMS RULER was ex-USS JOSEPH (AVG-50). Todd, Tacoma built twenty-one of the class, with one being built by the Puget Sound Navy Yard and one was built by Willamette and Commercial Iron Works.

The PRINCE WILLIAM (AVG-31) was 492 feet long with a 465 foot flight deck. The flight desk was 111 feet wide and 54 feet above the water. The deck was fitted with one catapult on the forward port side adjacent to the aircraft elevator. She had a beam of 69.6 feet and a draught of 23.3 feet. Displacement was rated at 7,800 tons standard and 13,000 tons fully loaded. Power was provided by two Foster-Wheeler boilers that produced a total of 8,500 horse power. She had two Westinghouse geared turbines which drove a single screw, giving the ship a rated speed of 17 knots and a range of 8,000 nautical miles at 15 knots.

Armament consisted of two 5 inch 38 caliber anti-aircraft guns, mounted in sponsons on each side of the fantail, ten 40MM Bofors twin mounts and twenty-seven 20MM Oerlikon anti-aircraft cannons mounted on either side of the flight deck.

The USS PRINCE WILLIAM served most of her active life as a aircraft transport in the Pacific area. In May of 1944, she was transferred to the Atlantic and used for carrier training and pilot qualifications in the Atlantic and Gulf of Mexico. One year later she was again returned to the Pacific for carrier training and aircraft transport duties. Following seven months of MAGIC CARPET operations, she again returned to the Atlantic, where she stayed until she was broken up in 1961, following service in the reserve fleet as a Helicopter Escort Carrier (CVHE).

All twenty-three of the British and the one Canadian PRINCE WILLIAM Class were officially returned to the U.S. Navy during 1945 and 1946 and stricken from the list of ships. The HMCS NABOB and HMS THANE were so badly damaged by German torpedoes that they were not returned.

The HMS EMPEROR was the former USS PYBUS (ACV-34) that was transferred to the British Royal Navy in 1943. When launched HMS EMPEROR was finished in Measure 22 camouflage, however, once in British service, Royal Navy camouflage was applied. HMS EMPEROR served primarily in the convoy escort role in the Atlantic. (Todd Shipyards)

A bow to stern view of hull number 30 under construction at Seattle-Tacoma Shipyards, Tacoma, Washington during October of 1942. The ship, which utilized a C-3 cargo type hull, would soon become the HMS AMEER, former USS BAFFINS (ACV-35). (Todd Shipyards)

A stern to bow view of the HMS RULER (hull number 45) under construction in building way number 2 at the Seattle-Tacoma Shipyards, Tacoma, Washington on 2 June 1943. The HMS RULER was the former USS ST JOSEPH (AVG-50) that was transferred to the Royal Navy. (Todd Shipyards)

There were twenty-four ships in the PRINCE WILLIAM class, but only one served with the U.S. Navy, the balance being used by the Royal Navy. The PRINCE WILLIAM (CVE-31) was used during the Second World War mainly as an aircraft transport. In late 1943 she was at sea carrying a deck load of twelve SBDs, an OS2U, two SOCs, a J2F and a R4D. (Elsilrac)

(Right) The HMS REAPER slides down the launching ways at Seattle-Tacoma Shipyards in November of 1943. The REAPER was completed in Royal Navy camouflage and was the former USS WINJAH. (Navy via Todd Shipyards)

The HMS AMEER underway in Commencement Bay, Washington during 1943. The HMS AMEER was finished in Measure 14 camouflage, however, this camouflage would soon be changed to a Royal Navy style camouflage scheme. (Todd Shipyards)

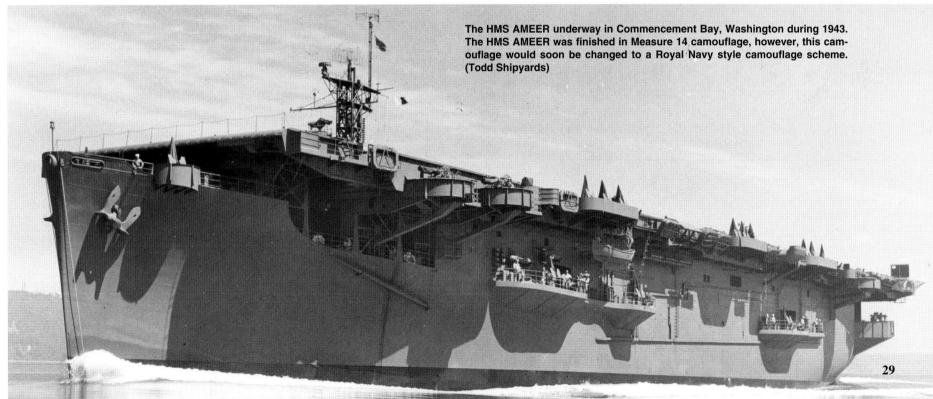

# CASABLANCA Class

The CASABLANCA Class represented an entirely new class of escort carriers. Henry J. Kaiser had obtained a contract from the Bureau of Ships (BuShips) to build fifty-five of the small carriers with the promise that the first four would be delivered by February of 1943, and the balance by the end of 1945. By utilizing the maritime commission S4-S2 BB-3 type high speed cargo hulls and a Gibbs & Cox marine design, Kaiser went to work building carriers at his shipyard in Vancouver, Washington. "Hurry up Henry," as he was called, fulfilled his promise and then some. The lead shop of the class, USS CASABLANCA (CVE-55) was commissioned on 8 July 1943 and the last, USS MUNDA (CVE-104) on 8 July 1944. All fifty ships had been commissioned within a year. All were destined for use by the U.S. Navy, although the USS SOLOMANS (CVE-67) was to have been sent to Britain as the HMS EMPEROR, however, the USS PYBUS (AVG-34) was sent instead. CVE-62 was laid down as the HMS BEGUM, but taken over by the U.S. Navy and renamed USS NATOMA BAY (CVE-62). Following this amazing feat of building speed, Kaiser was then given a contract to build eight escort carriers of the new COMMENCEMENT BAY Class.

The CASABLANCA Class ships were 498 feet 10 inches long with a beam of 65 feet. The hull on the CASABLANCA Class ships had a characteristic flat fantail, a good recognition feature of the class. The flight deck was 105 feet wide and 41 feet from the water. Two elevators, one fore and one aft and one catapult (fitted on the port side) were installed in the flight deck. The draught was 19 feet 8 inches and displacement was 6,730 tons standard and 10,200 tons fully loaded. Four boilers provided steam to the Skinner Unaflow reciprocating engine that produced 11,200 horse power driving twin screws, giving the class a rated speed of 19 knots and a range (with onboard fuel) of 10,200 nautical miles. The engine and boiler rooms were staggered to provide increased space for additional hanger area.

The armament consisted of one 5 inch 38 caliber anti-aircraft gun mounted in a tub on the fantail, eight 40MM twin mount Bofors cannons and twenty 20MM Oerlikon automatic cannons, mounted along either side of the flight deck in gun tubs. The CASABLANCA Class had the distinction of being the lightest armed of any combat escort carrier. This light weight anti-aircraft armament perhaps lead to the loss of USS BISMARCK SEA (CVE-95), USS OMMANEY BAY (CVE-79) and USS SAINT LO (CVE-63), all sunk by Japanese Kamikaze attacks in the Pacific. Two other CASABLANCA Class ships were lost to enemy action, USS GAMBLER BAY was lost to enemy gunfire during the Battle of Samar, Philippines and USS LISCOMBE BAY (CVE-56) was sunk by a torpedo from the Japanese fleet submarine I-175 off Tarawa.

The CASABLANCA Class wore four camouflage schemes during the war years: Measure 14, Ocean Gray (1943-44), Measure 21, Navy Blue system (1945), Measure 22, graded system (1944-45), Measure 32, medium pattern (1944), and Measure 33/10a, modified Thayer (light) system (1944-45). Measure 33 had been designed specifically for the CASABLANCA Class but was adapted to the SANGAMON Class CVEs and ESSEX Class CVs. Schemes were used both in the Atlantic and Pacific, unlike the BOGUE Class.

The majority of the CASABLANCA Class served in the Pacific with only five of their number serving in the Atlantic, mainly hunting German U-boats. The USS GUADALCANAL (CVE-60) had the distinction of being the only U.S. escort carrier to capture a U-boat intact. During an Atlantic cruise in the Summer of 1944, with Task Group 22.3, the GUADAL-CANAL's air group spotted the German U-505. During the next five days the Task Group

Originally laid down as the HMS AMEER and renamed USS ALAZON BAY in 1943, CVE-55 was once again renamed during 1945 as the USS CASABLANCA. The CASABLANCA served mainly in the training role in the Pacific. USS CASABLANCA, lead ship in a class of fifty ships, like all of her sisters, was constructed by Kaiser Shipbuilding, Vancouver, Washington. (Navy)

chased the sub until she was forced to surface during an intensive attack by the destroyer escort USS CHATERLAIN (DE-149) and aircraft from the GUADALCANAL. Once on the surface and helpless due to a stuck rudder, she was boarded and the American flag hoisted on her jack. For this action, the USS GUADALCANAL was awarded a Presidential Unit Citation. The U-505 is now on display at the Museum of Science and Industry in Chicago, Illinois.

In the Pacific, the action was hot and heavy with CASABLANCA Class ships fighting in every major battle during the island hopping campaigns. Kamikazes sunk three and damaged eleven, gunfire and Kamikazes, during the Battle of Samar, Philippines, damaged three more. Following the end of hostilities, CASABLANCA Class ships were used for MAGIC CARPET operations, bringing back U.S. servicemen. Most of the class that survived the war were put in the reserve fleet. Some were recalled for the Korean War and all were broken up by the 1960s.

The USS LISCOMBE BAY (CVE-56) served in the Pacific area during her short career. She is underway in the Pacific with a load of Douglas SBDs, Eastern TBMs and FMs aircraft on deck. The aircraft are undergoing an insignia change with bars being added to the star. The LISCOMBE BAY was sunk on 24 November 1943, by a Japanese submarine torpedo while operating off of the Gilbert Islands. (Navy)

The USS CORAL SEA (CVE-57) at sea during 1943 with VC-33, consisting of Eastern TBM bombers and FM fighters, assembled on the after flight deck. The CORAL SEA was originally named ALIKULA BAY, while on the building ways. She was again renamed, to USS ANZIO during 1944, and as the ANZIO, she was used in anti-submarine operations in the Pacific. (Navy)

The USS MISSION BAY (CVE-59) during August 1944 operating off the Atlantic coast. She is finished in Measure 32/4a camouflage and had at least six F6F Hellcats parked amidships on the flight deck. The MISSION BAY was used mainly in the anti-submarine role in the Atlantic. Both SK and SG radar antennas are fitted on the masts. (Navy)

## CASABLANCA Class, USS CASABLANCA (CVE-55)

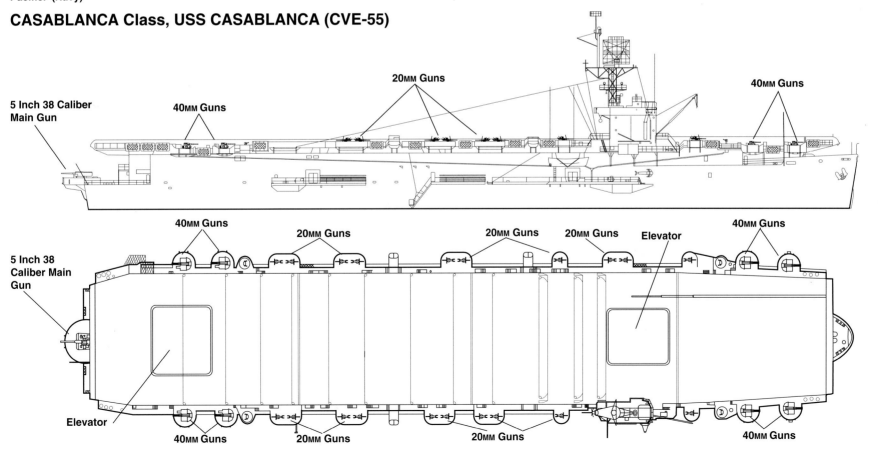

31

The USS GUADALCANAL (CVE-60) was one of the most highly decorated aircraft carriers of the Second World War. Her crew captured the German U-505 in the Atlantic during May of 1944. She was presented with a Presidential Unit Citation for her exploits in the Atlantic. (Navy)

The USS NATOMA BAY (CVE-62) underway in the Pacific during 1944, with her camouflage badly weathered. On 7 June 1945, USS NATOMA BAY was badly damaged by a Kamikaze attack, effectively putting her out of the Pacific war. (Navy)

Aircraft of VC-80 are positioned on the flight deck of USS MANILA BAY (CVE-61) prior to flight operations in 1944. The MANILA BAY could accommodate up to thirty-two aircraft in the hanger and on the flight deck. USS MANILA BAY would be involved in operations in the Pacific until damaged by a Kamikaze on 8 January 1945. Following repairs she returned to the Pacific. (Navy)

The USS MIDWAY (CVE-63) was renamed the USS ST LO on 15 September 1944. The name MIDWAY going to the new fleet carrier CVB-41. One month later a Kamikaze put the USS ST LO on the bottom of the Pacific during the Battle of Samar, Philippines. (Navy)

USS WAKE ISLAND (CVE-65) transporting aircraft of VC-8 to the Pacific area of operations. The WAKE ISLAND was finished in Measure 33/10a camouflage. USS WAKE ISLAND served both in the Atlantic and Pacific hunting submarines and transporting aircraft. (Navy)

A harbor tug positions the USS WHITE PLAINS (CVE-66) during 1944. The USS WHITE PLAINS was damaged by Kamikazes during the Battle of Samar in October 1944 and made a trip to Pearl Harbor for repairs. (Navy)

The USS TRIPOLI (CVE-64), being operated by the Maritime Sea Transport Service (MSTS), has a deck load of U.S. Air Force North American F-86D Sabre all-weather jet fighters during 1954. The TRIPOLI operated in both the Atlantic and Pacific during the Second World War. (Navy)

33

Flight operations are underway aboard USS NEHENTA BAY (CVE-74) during 1944, with Eastern aircraft FM Wildcats of VC-11 positioned on the forward flight deck. USS NEHENTA BAY operated in the Pacific, fighting in all of the major island hopping campaigns of the 1944-45 era. (Navy)

The USS OMMANEY BAY (CVE-79) operating in the waters off of Hawaii during 1944, with both aircraft elevators in the fully lowered position. The USS OMMANEY BAY was camouflaged in Measure 32/15a, the same scheme that she was wearing when she was sunk by a Kamikaze attack on 4 January 1945, off the Philippines. (Navy)

USS MARCUS ISLAND (CVE-77) was painted in Measure 32/15a during 1944. The variety of aircraft assembled on the deck indicates that she is being utilized as an aircraft transport. The paint shows a lot of weathering from salt exposure. (Navy)

The PETROF BAY (CVE-80) operating in the Pacific during 1944. finished in Measure 33/10a camouflage. The PETROF BAY was operating VC-76, a composite squadron that was comprised of TBM Avenger bombers and FM Wildcat fighter aircraft. A large SK radar antenna was fitted to the mast. (Navy)

## Anti-Aircraft Weapons

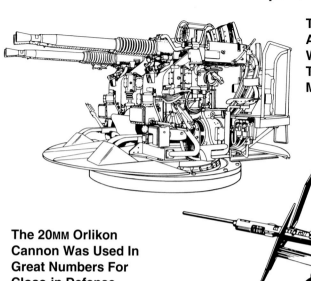

The 40MM Bofors Automatic Cannon Was Used In Both Twin And Quad Gun Mounts.

The 20MM Orlikon Cannon Was Used In Great Numbers For Close-in Defense. The Gun Could Be Mounted in Single Or Twin Mounts.

USS GAMBIER BAY (CVE-73) tied-up pier side during April of 1944. The GAMBIER BAY was sunk by the Japanese battleship YAMATO during the Battle of Samar, Philippines on 25 October 1944. That was the only loss of an escort carrier to naval surface vessels during the Second World War. (Navy)

USS SITKOH BAY (T-CVE-86) at sea transporting a variety of aircraft during the Korean war. The designator, T, was added to her designation to signify her role as a transport-escort carrier. The deck load consisted of TBM, SNB, R4D, JD and F4U aircraft. The USS SITKOF BAY had also been used mainly as a aircraft transport during the Second World War. (Navy)

The USS SHIPLEY BAY (CVE-85), with VC-97 FM Wildcats on the bow, steams into the wind recovering aircraft (as indicated by the LSO wind screen on the after flight deck). The SHIPLEY BAY was camouflaged in Measure 22, which consisted of Navy Gray and Haze Gray. (Navy)

## 5 Inch 38 Caliber Main Gun

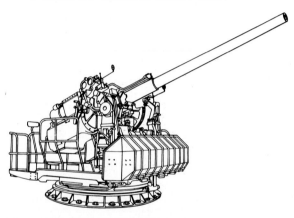

The USS SAVO ISLAND (CVE-78) underway with a deck load of various aircraft and aircraft parts. A J2F Duck minus its engine is parked adjacent to the island. In January of 1945, the SAVO ISLAND was damaged by a Kamikaze attack off the Philippines. Repaired, she rejoined the fleet in time for the Battle of Okinawa in March of 1945. (Navy)

The USS STEAMER BAY (CVE-87) is maneuvered into its anchorage position during late 1944. Her Measure 32/12a camouflage was badly weathered from salt exposure. The STEAMER BAY was damaged in an collision with USS HALE (DD-642) in April 1945 and by an aircraft accident in June of 1945 and had to put into Guam for repairs. (Navy)

The USS SARGENT BAY (CVE-83) rides at anchor while the crew make repairs to the bridge canvas cover. The SARGENT BAY was camouflaged in Measure 32/15a. A protective railing was fitted around both the forward and after elevators. The rear elevator has just received a fresh coat of paint as indicated by the unfinished 83. (Navy)

The USS TAKANIS BAY (CVE-89) underway at high speed in the Pacific during May of 1944. The TAKANIS BAY operated as a training carrier for pilot qualifications during the later part of the Second World War and was camouflaged in Measure 14, the Ocean Gray system. (Navy)

## 3 Inch 50 Caliber Secondary Armament

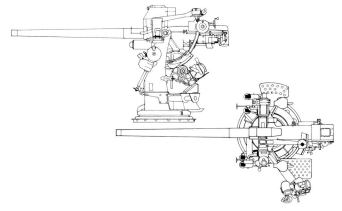

The USS CAPE ESPERANCE (CVE-88) bound for Korea with Air Force F-84s, F-86s, T-6s and F-80s, along with an Army L-20 and Navy F6F on deck. During the Korean war the CAPE ESPERANCE was operated by a civilian MSTS crew. The only Navy men onboard were the crew of the 5 inch gun on the fantail. (Navy)

Aircraft of VC-84 prepare to take off from USS MAKIN ISLAND (CVE-93) during early 1945. VC-84 provided air support with their TBM and FM aircraft during the invasions of Leyte and Luzon. The prominent square antenna on the mast was the SK search radar antenna. (Navy)

The USS WINDHAM BAY (CVE-92) sails into harbor during 1945. The starboard forward twin 40MM guns are in the full vertical position. The deck load consisted of at least three Martin P5M Mariners. The WINDHAM BAY was used for aircraft transport duties during the Second World War. (Navy)

The USS KWAJALEIN (CVE-98) at sea operating as an aircraft transport with six OS2U Kingfishers occupying the after flight deck. The catapult area has been covered over as have the 40MM guns indicating that she was outside the combat zone. A round SK-2 radar was fitted to the mast. (Navy)

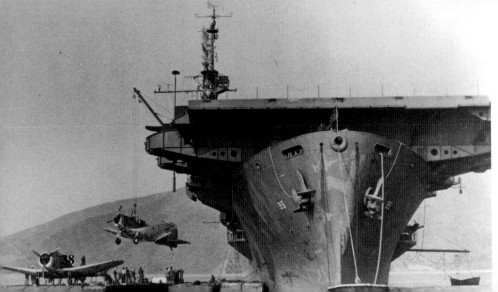

(Left) The USS BISMARK SEA (CVE-95) unloads a pair of SBD Dauntless dive bombers at Iwo Jima, during February of 1945. On 21 February 1945, the BISMARK SEA was sunk by a Kamikaze off of Iwo Jima with the loss of 318 killed. (Navy)

The USS LUNGA POINT (CVE-94) with a TBM about to be catapulted off the forward deck. The aircraft are from VC-85 which was assigned to the ship during early 1945. The LUNGA POINT was damaged by a Kamikaze on 21 February 1945 off Iwo Jima. (Navy)

The USS ATTU (CVE-102) was used to transport aircraft to Iwo Jima and Okinawa during the later stages of the Pacific war. Following hostilities she was used to transport men and materials home as part of Operation MAGIC CARPET. (Navy)

The USS MATANIKAU (CVE-101) at sea in the Pacific area operating with Carrier Transport Squadron, Pacific during July of 1944. The MATANIKAU was finished in Measure 21, the Navy Blue system. The MATANIKAU also operated as a training carrier for pilot qualifications. (Navy)

The USS MUNDA (CVE-104) was the last ship in the CASABLANCA class. USS MUNDA operated with Carrier Transport Squadron, Pacific, bringing much needed aircraft and spare parts to the Pacific combat zone. Her hull number, 104, was painted on both the bow and the island. (Navy)

# COMMENCEMENT BAY Class

The COMMENCEMENT BAY Class represented the last class of escort carriers built for service in the Second World War. A total of twenty-seven were ordered from Todd Shipbuilding and eight from Kaiser, although only nineteen were actually constructed, all by Todd, Pacific. The contract with Kaiser and Todd, for the balance of the ships, was canceled on 11 August 1945.

The COMMENCEMENT BAY Class was built using a modified SANGAMON type hull with modifications gained by war experiences with the former classes. Ships of the COMMENCEMENT BAY Class were 553 feet long, with a seventy-five foot beam. The flight deck was 105 foot wide and 503 feet long, fitted with two catapults on the forward deck and two aircraft elevators. Draught was 30 feet 7 inches and displacement was rated at 12,000 tons standard and 23,875 tons fully loaded. The engine rooms were staggered so that the maximum size boilers could be installed. All had four boilers that provided steam to the geared turbines. The machinery produced 16,000 horse power driving twin screws, giving the COMMENCEMENT BAY Class a maximum speed of 18 knots. An onboard fuel capacity of 3,134 tons gave them a range of some 8,000 miles at a cruising speed of 15 knots.

The ships of the COMMENCEMENT BAY Class were armed with two 5 inch 38 caliber guns mounted on the fantail, although a few of the class were fitted with a single 5 inch 38 caliber weapon just forward of the island in a tub usually occupied by a twin 40MM mount. Other weapons included three 40MM quad mounts, twelve 40MM twin mounts, and twenty 20MM Orliekon cannons. Various radar types were carried, the most common being the SK-2 sea search, SPS-4/SG range/bearing, and YE aircraft homing beacon radar. Up to thirty aircraft could be carried and handled, usually Grumman F6F and Chance-Vought F4U fighters and TBF/TBM Avengers. Air groups from both the Navy and Marine Corps operated from COMMENCEMENT BAY Class ships.

The COMMENCEMENT BAY Class, those that had been commissioned, served exclusively in the Pacific area of operations. CVE-105 through 113 were used either as training carriers, air cover for invasions or as aircraft transports. Following the war, most were put in the reserve fleet, awaiting to be needed again to take the fight to an enemy. They didn't have long to wait. On 25 June 1950, forces from Communist North Korea burst across the border separating North and South Korea and U.S. forces were again called to a war time footing. First into action was the USS SICILY (CVE-118) with VMF-214 The Blacksheep Squadron. On 3 August 1950, the first marine air strike was carried out by VMF-214 against positions in South Korea held by North Korean troops. VMF-323 flying off of the USS BADOENG STRAIT (CVE-116) joined the fight a short time later. Also entering the combat zone was USS RENDOVA (CVE-114) with VMF-212 Devil Cats, USS BAIROKO (CVE-115) with VMF-312 Checkerboards and VMA-332. USS POINT CURZ (CVE-119) with VS-38 provided anti-submarine protection. Following the Korean War, the ships of the COMMENCEMENT BAY Class were again put in the reserve fleet.

During 1961, the USS GILBERT ISLAND (CVE-107) was selected for conversion into a major communications ship. The conversion, which took place at New York Navy Yard, included the removal of all aircraft handling equipment, modification of the bow area, and the installation of radio antenna towers. Four twin mounted radar controlled 3 inch 50 caliber anti-aircraft cannons were installed on the edge of the deck. Once the conversion was completed the ship was re-commissioned as the USS ANNAPOLIS (AGMR-1). During the

**The USS COMMENCEMENT BAY (CVE-105) was the leader of the class of nineteen escort carriers. During the Second World War USS COMMENCEMENT BAY was used mainly as a training carrier for deck and air crews. (Elsilrac)**

Vietnam era the COMMENCEMENT BAY Class along with four members of the BOGUE Class, were again called upon to serve, this time designated as AKVs, Aircraft Transport, Auxiliary. USS KULA GULF, CAPE GLOUCESTER, RENDOVA, POINT CURZ, 40 and COMMENCEMENT BAY were all used to transport aircraft needed to supply the needs of the U.S. Army, Air Force and Marines in Southeast Asia. By 1972, all of the COMMENCEMENT BAY Class had been decommissioned and sold for scrap; having. served their country with great honor.

**A hapless pilot from VS-22 flying from USS BLOCK ISLAND crashed his Grumman AF-2 Guardian into the water. He was rescued by a Piasecki HUP helicopter of HU-2. The BLOCK ISLAND served during the Korean war era, operating in the Atlantic. (Elsilrac)**

Flight operations are about to commence aboard USS GILBERT ISLAND (CVE-107) as an Eastern TBM-3 spreads its wings. The flight deck contains Marine Corps F6F, TBM and F4U aircraft. The GILBERT ISLAND would later be converted into a major radio communications ship and renamed the USS ANNAPOLIS (AGMR-1). (Elsilrac)

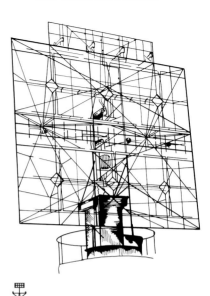

## SK Search Radar

## COMMENCEMENT BAY Class, USS COMMENCEMENT BAY (CVE-105)

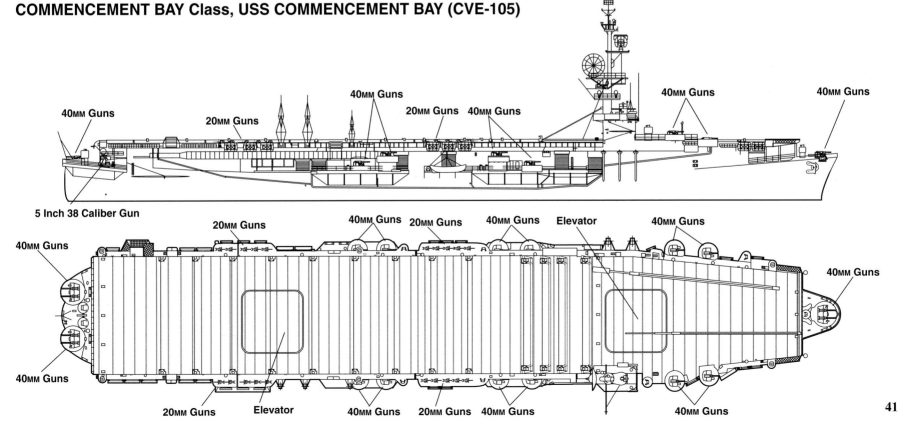

40мм Guns
20мм Guns
40мм Guns
20мм Guns 40мм Guns
40мм Guns
40мм Guns
5 Inch 38 Caliber Gun

40мм Guns
20мм Guns
40мм Guns 20мм Guns 40мм Guns Elevator 40мм Guns
40мм Guns
40мм Guns
40мм Guns
20мм Guns Elevator 40мм Guns 20мм Guns 40мм Guns 40мм Guns

The USS SALERNO BAY (CVE-110) was finished in Measure 21 camouflage just before her commissioning in 1945. The SALERNO BAY would go on to serve in the Pacific during the Second World War and in the Atlantic and Mediterranean during the Korean War era. She was withdrawn from service during 1954. (Elsilrac)

(Right) The USS VELLA GULF (CVE-111) was used near the end of the war in the Western Pacific off Okinawa and the Japanese home islands. During the war she carried a Marine air group that consisted of F4U, F6F and TBM aircraft. (Elsilrac)

The USS KULA GULF (CVE-108) underway with F4U Corsairs on the after flight deck during 1950. The KULA GULF was used for pilot training and as an aircraft transport during the Korean era. Following the Korean war she was used for development work in anti-submarine warfare methods and tactics. (Elsilrac)

USS CAPE GLOUCESTER (CVE-109) was used at the very end of the war in the Pacific for Kamikaze defense off the coast of Japan. Following the war she was used to return American GI's home as part of Operation MAGIC CARPET during 1945. The CAPE GLOUCESTER was camouflaged in Measure 22. (Elsilrac)

The USS SIBONEY (CVE-112) at sea with TBM-3s of VS-32 on the flight deck and a HO3S on the stern. The HO3S would act as a plane guard once flight operations commenced. The TBM-3s were operated in the anti-submarine role during 1953. The SIBONEY served in the Atlantic ocean during the Korean era. (Elsilrac)

USS PUGET SOUND (CVE-113) at sea on builders trials during 1945. Finished in Measure 22, she would serve in the Western Pacific off Okinawa and Japan. Following the war she was sent to the Atlantic for duty with the reserve fleet. She was reactivated during Korea for Atlantic operations. (Elsilrac)

USS BADOENG STRAIGHT (CVE-116) with F4Us of VMF-212 off the Korean coast on 13 January 1952. The BADOENG STRAIGHT had three operational periods off Korea during the 1950-1953 period. A F4U is on the port catapult ready for takeoff on a ground support mission. (Elsilrac)

The USS BAIROKO (CVE-115) enters port with a F4U from CVG-15 on the flight deck. The BAIROKO participated in the hydrogen bomb tests in January of 1954 off Eniwetok. During the tests it was discovered that by spraying salt water on the deck that the effects of the radiation were greatly reduced. (Elsilrac)

USS SAIDOR (CVE-117) on builders trials during 1946. Built to late to see action in the Second World War, she served in the Pacific and participated in the Bikini atomic bomb test acting as a photographic laboratory documenting the atomic blast. (Elsilrac)

44

The USS RENDOVA (CVE-114) underway in the Pacific with nine F4U Corsairs from VMF-334 on her flight deck. VMF-334 embarked in USS RENDOVA during the Korean war era. RENDOVA also embarked VMF-212 during her 1951 Korean cruise and, during 1952, she participated in the Marshall Island atomic bomb tests. (Elsilrac)

USS MINDORO (CVE-120) with airship K-69 taking off from her deck during carrier landing and takeoff qualifications on 28 April 1950. The K-69 was a non-rigid patrol airship used in anti-submarine operations. USS MINDORO was used as a training carrier and had all her defensive armament removed. (Elsilrac)

## SC Radar

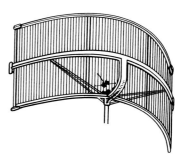

45

The USS SICILY (CVE-118) was repainted with new deck markings designed to show a landing pilot the centerline of the flight deck. The SICILY, with VMF-214 Blacksheep, was the first Navy unit to attack North Korean positions on 3 August 1950. USS SICILY sailed to Korea three times in support of United Nations forces from 1950 to 1953. (Elsilrac)

USS SICILY underway off Korea closely followed by a plane guard destroyer escort during 1950. The SICILY's twin converging catapults are visible on the forward flight deck. The mast contains SPS-6, SP and YE radar antennas. (Navy via NMNA)

USS SICILY with F4U-4s of VMF-214 on the forward flight deck. Captain John S. Thach commanded the SICILY from June 1950 until relieved in August of 1951. Captain Thach became famous during the Second World War for his Thach "weave," an maneuver used by F4F pilots that was successful against Japanese Zero fighters. (Navy via NMNA)

Grumman TBM-3E Avengers of VS-38 are parked on the flight deck of the USS POINT CRUZ (CVE-119) awaiting flight orders. The POINT CRUZ operated off of Korea during 1953 in the anti-submarine role. She would go on to serve during the Vietnam conflict operating as an aircraft transport. (Elsilrac)

The USS PALAU (CVE-122) was completed to late for Second World War service. During the post war period she served mainly in the Atlantic before being placed in reserve. During the Korean war era she was reactivated for service in the Atlantic and Mediterrain area in the anti-submarine role. (Elsilrac)

The USS TINIAN (CVE-123) at sea during builders trials in 1946. She was the last ship of the COMMENCEMENT BAY class to be commissioned. The TINIAN served her time in the reserve fleet until she was stricken in 1970. (Elsilrac)

# Conversions

Beginning in June of 1955, the U.S. Navy began converting the THETIS BAY, then designated as a CVE, to an Assault Helicopter Transport (CVHA) for use by the Marine Corps. The conversion took place at the San Francisco Naval Shipyard and once completed, the THETIS BAY was commissioned as CVHA-1 and placed under the command of Amphibious Force, Pacific. The conversion included shortening the aft flight deck to expose the aft elevator, removal of the after gun tub that contained the 5 inch 38 caliber anti-aircraft gun and elimination of catapult and arresting gear, since they were not required for helicopter operations. During 1959 the USS THETIS BAY was redesignated as an Amphibious Assault Ship and designated LPH-6. On 1 March 1964, the THETIS BAY was withdrawn from service and while transfer to Spain was considered, the USS CABOT (CVL-28) was sent instead.

On 27 October 1964, the National Aeronautics and Space Administration (NASA) borrowed the USNS CROATAN (ex-CVE-25) for use as a floating rocket launching pad. NASA added an Arcas meteorological rocket launcher tube to the fantail area and two Nike-Apache rail-type launchers along side the after elevator. Radar vans and tracking antennas were added to the forward flight deck area. The hanger deck was utilized for the operations and tracking equipment vans. Once all modifications were completed, the CROATAN, operated by Military Sealift Command, sailed to the Equator area off the west coast of South America to participate in the 1964-65 International Quiet Sun Year. During the cruise, some seventy-seven scientific experiments were launched. Following her use by NASA the CROATAN was returned to the Navy and stricken during 1970.

The third major conversion of a CVE involved USS GILBERT ISLAND (CVE-107). Stricken on 1 June 1961, the GILBERT ISLAND was reactivated in November and sailed to New York Shipyard for her conversion into a major Communications Relay Ship (AGMR). The modifications involved the removal of all catapult and arresting gear, as well as the 5 inch 38 caliber, 40MM and 20MM anti-aircraft guns, these were replaced by four radar controlled twin 3 inch 50 caliber weapons, two to port and two to starboard. The flight deck mounted four tall radio antennas and the hanger deck area contained the radio vans housing twenty-four radio transmitters. A helicopter landing pad was placed on the port side of the deck.

Following conversion, the GILBERT ISLAND was recommissioned as the USS ANNAPOLIS (AGMR-1) after the U.S. Navy radio base there. The USS ANNAPOLIS served in the Pacific area in support of U.S. forces in Vietnam. Following her Vietnam service, she was withdrawn and placed in the reserve fleet. USS ANNAPOLIS was stricken on 15 October 1976, having been replaced by the BLUE RIDGE Class of amphibious command ships.

**The USS THETIS BAY (CVE-90) was converted to an assault helicopter aircraft carrier for the Marine Corps and redesignated as CVHA-1. The THETIS BAY was used as an aircraft transport and helicopter assault ship from 1956 until redesignated as an Amphibious Assault Ship (LPH-6) during 1956. She was finally withdrawn from service on 1 March 1964 The aircraft visible just in front of the island is a North American AJ Savage attack bomber. (Elsilrac)**

USS THETIS BAY now designated as LPH-6 operating in shallow water during 1959. The circles on the deck indicate the helicopter landing and staging areas. The conversion to CVHA/LPH involved the shortening of the after flight deck, the removal of the stern gun tub and double decking the island structure. (Elsilrac)

A stern view of the USS CROATAN shows the Nike launchers positioned next to the after aircraft elevator and the vertical launch tube for the ARCAS meteorological rocket. The USS CROATAN participated in NASA's Quiet Sun 1964-65 experiments off the Western coast of South America. Once the experiments were completed the CROATAN was returned to the Navy and redesignated as AKV-25. (NASA)

The USNS CROATAN (CVE-25) was loaned to the National Aeronautical and Space Administration (NASA) in 1964 and the flight deck was converted to fire experimental rockets. The flight deck was covered with antennas, radio/radar vans and rocket launching equipment. (NASA)

The USS ANNAPOLIS (AGMR-1) was converted from the former USS GILBERT ISLAND (CVE-107). The USS ANNAPOLIS was a major communications relay ship that was used during the Vietnam era relaying messages from command centers in-country Vietnam back to the national command authority in Washington. The conversion from CVE to AGMR involved the modification of the flight deck with a hurricane bow, deletion of the Second World War armament and the addition of four radar controlled twin 3 inch 50 anti-aircraft gun mounts, two per side. (Naval History Center)

The USS ANNAPOLIS (AGMR-1) was used off the coast of Vietnam from 1965 to 1969, when she was withdrawn from service. As a major communications ship she was used to relay radio messages from on and off shore Vietnam back to the United States. The flight deck housed four large radio antennas and a helicopter pad. When not operating in the Vietnam war zone, ANNAPOLIS was home-ported in San Diego, California. (National Archives)